Contents

Any words appearing in the text in bold, **like this**, are explained in the Glossary.

Communication

Communication lets people in different places talk to each other. It tells us about things that happen in other countries. It also helps entertain us.

What is television?

Television, newspapers, telephone, post, the **Internet** and radio are all forms of communication. You can watch many different programmes on television.

You can watch television programmes from all over the world in your own house.

This is the view from the back of a television **studio**. You can see the **camera operators** who do the filming. There are many other people who help to make a television programme.

Some programmes are for entertainment, like cartoons, comedies, sports and game shows. Some are about news, science or history.

This book tells you about how television programmes are made. It also explains how the programmes reach you.

Television stations

A television station makes television programmes. The television station also sends the programmes out to your television. This is called **broadcasting**.

There are thousands of television stations around the world. Local television stations broadcast to people in a town or a city. National television stations broadcast to everyone in a country. International television stations broadcast to many countries.

Each television station has its own special symbol. Many stations show this symbol on the screen so you always know what channel you are watching.

These people are planning a television programme. This can be a complicated job.

Making programmes

Many people get programmes ready to broadcast. **Journalists** find news stories for news programmes. Writers, actors and make-up artists are all needed to make a drama programme.

Television programmes are made up of moving pictures and sounds. **Camera operators** film the pictures and sound engineers **record** the sounds. The pictures and sounds are sent to a machine called a **transmitter**. This sends programmes from the station to the viewers.

Gathering news

Journalists work in a large office called a newsroom. News stories come in all day. The journalists work quickly to get news to the viewers.

Most television stations show a main news programme in the evening. News **journalists** make and present this programme. Some journalists only work on one subject, such as sports.

Some stories come from news agencies. These companies find news stories and send them to television and radio stations and to newspapers.

This **camera operator** is using a video camera to take pictures and a **microphone** to record sounds. The reporter is interviewing the man on the right.

Editors and reporters

News **editors** choose the stories for news programmes. Reporters try to find information about the stories. They go to the scene of a story with a camera crew.

A news story

Imagine that there is a big flood. A news editor decides to send a reporter and camera crew. The reporter interviews people whose homes have been flooded. The camera crew films the flood.

Television pictures

The picture on your screen is a moving picture made up of lots of pictures, like photographs. Each still picture is called a frame.

Twenty-five frames appear every second. This is so fast that your brain can't see the frames changing.

How a television camera works

A television camera takes the moving pictures that you see on television. It takes 25 pictures every second.

Cameras in **studios** are put on tripods, like the one above, to keep the picture steady while filming.

The camera collects light rays coming from the scene the camera is pointing at. It makes a small picture of the scene.

The camera turns the picture into an electrical **signal** 25 times a second. This signal is like a copy of the picture in electricity. If the signal is sent to a television set, a moving picture of the scene appears on the screen.

This is the view the **camera operator** sees through the camera. The operator can **zoom** in and out to make things look bigger or smaller.

Storing pictures

If a camera **records** the pictures, they can be looked at later. Recorded television pictures are stored on video tape or on a computer.

Recording pictures

When a video camera is recording, it puts the **signal** from the camera on to tape. When the video tape is played, the video machine reads the signal on the tape.

This **camera operator** is filming with a **digital** video camera. The pictures can be stored on digital cassette or sent back to the **studio** for a **live broadcast**.

Editing

Imagine that a camera crew have filmed a flood. The recorded film is going to be shown on a news programme.

An **editor** chooses which pictures to use in the news report about the flood. He or she then uses an **editing** machine to cut out the unwanted pictures.

This is the editing room at a television station. The people are editing pictures and sounds to make them ready to be shown.

Television studios

The place where a programme is made is called a **studio**. A news programme is made in part of the studio called the set. This is where the **presenter** works. A news programme has its own studio and set.

Studio equipment

Studios have lots of equipment. There are cameras, **microphones** to **record** voices and bright lights to light up the set.

This weather map on the screen is created in a computer. The map is put behind the presenter electronically. He is really standing in front of a plain blue screen.

This is a control room in a television studio. Each screen has a label to show which camera its pictures are coming from.

The control room

The pictures from the cameras go to a **control room**. They appear on screens called monitors. There is one monitor for each camera. Sounds from the microphones also go to the control room.

In the control room there are machines for playing recorded tapes. There are also computers that can do tricks with the pictures, such as turn them upside down.

Broadcasting news

Here is the timetable for a half-hour news programme. It is called a running order. It shows the length of each part of the programme and who presents it.

On the front of each camera is an **autocue**. The newsreader looks into the camera and reads the words on the autocue.

Time (mins : secs)	Programme section
00.00	Opening music
00.30	News summary (newsreader)
03.30	Live news report (reporter)
05.00	**Recorded** advertisements
07.00	Recorded news report (reporter)
08.00	News in brief (newsreader)
09.00	News interview (newsreader)
11.00	Recorded advertisements
13.00	News summary (newsreader)
15.30	Sports news (sports reporter)
18.30	Recorded advertisements
20.00	Recorded news report (reporter)
23.00	News interview (newsreader)
25.00	Weather (weather **presenter**)
27.00	Headlines (newsreader)
29.30	**Credits**
30.00	Programme ends

Directing the programme

The **director** in the **control room** decides which pictures the viewers see. A person called a vision mixer changes from one picture to another. A sound mixer works the controls that switch between different sounds.

The newsreader reads off the autocue. He gets messages about what news story is next through a small **microphone** in his ear.

Other programmes

Programmes like game shows are often pre-recorded. This means they are **recorded** then shown on television later. A game show needs lots of preparation. Researchers have to work out questions. Writers write the words for the **presenter**. Other people choose people to play and invite an audience.

During a game show, **camera operators** move their cameras around the studio. They can **zoom** in to show the presenter or one of the players.

A television van at an outside broadcast has a dish on top. This sends pictures from the cameras back to the television station.

During the game show, the pictures from the cameras and the sounds from the **microphones** are recorded. They are then **edited** to make the final programme that you see on your television.

Outside broadcasts

An outside **broadcast** is a programme made outside a **studio**. Outside broadcasts include sports events and musical concerts. Pictures from the cameras at the outside broadcast go to a small **control room** inside a van. Then they are sent back to the television station.

Pictures

There are three ways that pictures are **broadcast** from television stations.

Cable television

In **cable** television, the pictures are sent from a television station to televisions by electricity. The electricity travels along underground cables. Sometimes the pictures travel by light using **optical-fibre cables** instead of electricity.

A television cable is being put under the ground. The cable will carry telephone calls as well as television pictures.

Terrestrial television

In **terrestrial** television, the pictures travel from a television station to your television by **radio waves**. A television station sends out the waves and your television collects them.

Satellite television

There are **satellites** high up in space. Television stations send pictures to the satellites using powerful radio waves called microwaves. The satellite sends the pictures down to your television.

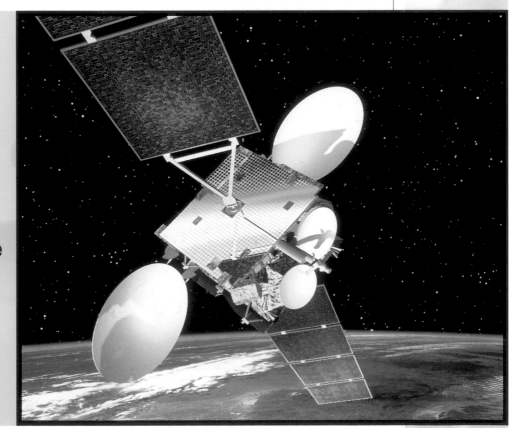

Satellites like this one send television pictures around the world.

Sending signals

This is how pictures are sent out in **terrestrial** television. Television cameras make **signals** that go to the **control room** at the television station. From here the signals are sent to a **transmitter**.

The transmitter turns the signals into **radio waves**. The waves then carry the pictures to your television. The waves spread out from the transmitter mast like waves spread out in a pond when you drop a stone in.

The transmitter is at the very top of this mast. The signals can reach a wider area than if the transmitter were at ground level.

Picking a station

The television stations send pictures using different radio waves. You can change channels to get waves from different stations.

Some new televisions are **digital**. The pictures are always very clear and there are many more channels to choose from.

On this digital television you can watch the newsreader read news stories. You can read stories on the screen yourself as well.

Television sets

Your television set turns the waves from the television stations back into moving pictures and sounds.

Collecting pictures

The television set collects the waves using a metal rod or wire called an aerial. You need special boxes and **satellite** dishes to receive **cable** and satellite television.

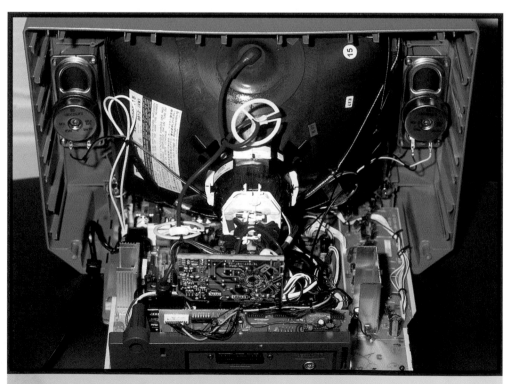

A television set with the back taken off. You can see the big glass tube where the picture is made. There are speakers on each side of the screen.

Inside the television

Inside most television sets there is a big piece of glass shaped like a vase. The screen that you look at is the wide end of this. On the back of the screen there are thousands of coloured dots.

A machine at the other end of the shaped glass sends beams at the screen. When the beams hit the dots, the dots glow, making up the picture that you see.

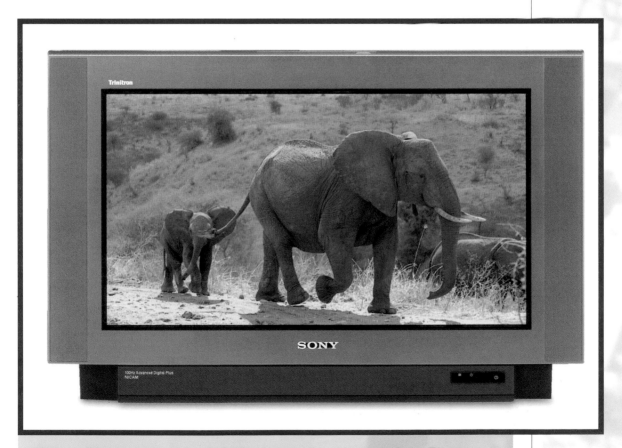

Flat, widescreen televisions have no glass tube. They can even be hung on the wall like paintings.

Modern machines

Up until the 1980s, people could only watch television programmes on their televisions. The **Internet** did not exist then.

Modern communication

Now you can surf the Internet on a television. On your computer you can listen to the radio, make telephone calls and watch television.

You can find out all sorts of information on your television by using the Internet.

These people are having a meeting with people in another town or country. They can see them on the screen. The people on the screen can see and hear them too.

Some televisions have a computer inside that **records** programmes. The computer learns which programmes are your favourites. It automatically records them for you.

Different sorts of communications are getting mixed together. By the year 2010 there might be a machine at home that is a television, a telephone, a computer and a radio all in one.

Television times

Here are some important events in the history of television.

1884 In Germany, Paul Nipkow invents the Nipkow disc. When the disc spins round, it works like a simple television camera.

1923 In the USA, Vladimir Zworykin invents a glass tube that takes television pictures.

1926 In Britain, John Logie Baird demonstrates the first television system. It uses a Nipkow disc.

1929 The first-ever television pictures are **broadcast** by the British Broadcasting Corporation (BBC).

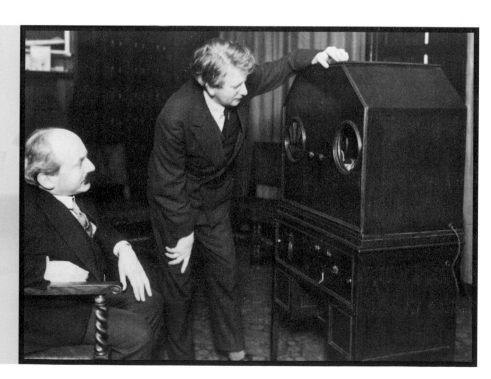

John Logie Baird showing the first working television system in 1926. The screen is the round hole on the right side of the box.

1936 Television is broadcast every day by the BBC.

1939 The first television broadcasts are made in the USA.

1953 The first-ever colour pictures are broadcast.

1956 The first video recorder for **recording** pictures is built in the USA.

1962 Television pictures are broadcast from the USA to Europe by **satellite**.

1999 Televisions that can be used to surf the **Internet** are made.

This is what a television studio looked like in 1953. The man on the right is working a television camera. There is a **microphone** at the top.

Glossary

autocue special screen on the front of a television camera with the words on it the presenter needs to read

broadcast make and send out television programmes. A broadcast is a television programme.

cable way of broadcasting pictures along cables underground

camera operator person who works a television camera

control room room in a television station where the pictures and sounds are checked

credits list of people who have helped make a television programme

digital something that uses signals that can be read by computers

director person in charge of a programme or studio

edit cut out unwanted pictures and sounds

editor person who decides what goes in a programme

Internet huge network of computers that stretches right around the world

journalist person who finds out and makes programmes about the news

live pictures or sounds broadcast at the same time as they are made

microphone something that collects sounds and turns them into a signal

optical-fibre cable cable with thin threads of glass inside. Flashes of light travel along the threads.

presenter person who appears on a television programme, such as the person who asks questions on a quiz programme

radio waves invisible waves that travel through air, space and many other objects

record store pictures or sounds on tapes or computers

satellite object in space that orbits around the Earth

signal electric current that represents a television picture

studio room where television programmes are made

terrestrial way of broadcasting pictures by radio waves

transmitter machine that sends out television programmes

zoom change the camera lens to make something look close or far away

Index

www.heinemann.co.uk/library
Visit our website to find out more information about **Heinemann Library** books.

To order:
☎ Phone ++44 (0)1865 888066
📄 Send a fax to ++44 (0)1865 314091
💻 Visit the Heinemann Bookshop at www.heinemann.co.uk/library to browse our catalogue and order online.

First published in Great Britain by Heinemann Library, Halley Court, Jordan Hill, Oxford OX2 8EJ, a division of Reed Educational and Professional Publishing Ltd. Heinemann is a registered trademark of Reed Educational & Professional Publishing Ltd.

OXFORD MELBOURNE AUCKLAND JOHANNESBURG BLANTYRE
GABORONE IBADAN PORTSMOUTH NH (USA) CHICAGO

Designed by Visual Image
Originated by Ambassador Litho Ltd.
Printed in Hong Kong/China

06 05 04 03 02   06 05 04 03 02
10 9 8 7 6 5 4 3 2 1   10 9 8 7 6 5 4 3 2 1
ISBN 0431 11282 7 (hardback)   ISBN 0431 11289 4 (paperback)

British Library Cataloguing in Publication Data

Oxlade, Chris
    Television. – (In touch)
    1. Television – Juvenile literature
    I. Title
    621.3'88

Acknowledgements

The Publishers would like to thank the following for permission to reproduce photographs:
Associated Press: pp14, 27; Bush Internet: p26; Corbis: pp5, 8, 17, 20, 22, 28; David Hoffman: p19; Hulton Getty: p29; Liz Eddison: p12; Norman Osborne: p18; Pearson TV: pp7, 13, 18; R.D. Battersby: p24; Robert Harding: p11; Science Photo Library: p21; Sky News: p23; Sky, ABC, BBC, ITN: p6; Sony: p10; Stone: p15, Elie Bernager p4, Bob Thomas p9.

Cover photograph reproduced with permission of Stone.

Every effort has been made to contact copyright holders of any material reproduced in this book. Any omissions will be rectified in subsequent printings if notice is given to the Publisher.

In Touch

Television

Chris Oxlade

Heinemann
LIBRARY